Strategically relevant

Your optimal workplace culture and the leadership to create it.

How to identify, lead and create your optimal workplace culture — strategic and relevant — that delights customers, engages employees, supports execution and achieves results.

Philip Oude-Vrielink

ISBN 978-0-9875222-4-5
1. Corporate culture.   2. Organizational behaviour.   3. Organizational change.   4. Leadership.   5. Strategy.   I. Oude-Vrielink, Philip.   II. Title.

National Library of Australia Cataloguing-in-Publication entry:
Oude-Vrielink, Philip, author.

Strategically relevant : Your optimal workplace culture and the leadership to create it / Philip Oude-Vrielink.

ISBN 9780987522245 (paperback)

Corporate culture.

Organizational behaviour.
Organizational change.

Leadership.
302.35

Cover photo by Philip Oude-Vrielink
Cover design by Lucy Hardie

May you
manifest even more
of your magnificence

Table of contents

About the author

Philip Oude-Vrielink is a passionate and illuminating individual specialising in the fields of leadership, culture and change.

He holds a degree in Biomedical and Communications Engineering, has a graduate diploma in Organisational Dynamics, decades of corporate change experience, and is an insight and mindfulness facilitator. This gives him an effective and practical integrative openness, non-judgemental presence and useful depth.

Through his career, he has worked in large systems design, project and change management, business transformation, leadership development and culture change.

His focus is on helping people lead, live and create what's important, to answer what their lives are the answer to and be more authentic, purposeful and fulfilled. He has 25 years experience helping people be more effective and influential, create more effective organisations and cultures, and have greater fulfilment and success in their lives.

Philip runs programs helping good people, change agents, thought leaders, and business leaders live lives that are personally and commercially more effective, authentic and purposeful. For organisations, Philip runs *The Aware Leader*, *Important Conversations*, *Group Value*, and *Leading Legacy* leadership development programs, and a range of integrated programs that support complete culture transformation and development. Publicly, he runs *Conversations That Connect* and *Life On Purpose* private mentoring programs.

An educator at heart, Phil is obsessed with helping people bring their values to life and create what's important — for themselves and others. With an enthusiastic ability for keeping people engaged and challenged enough to keep growing, he brings clarity, focus and skilful action to individuals and organisational leadership.

He has one criterion for assessing usefulness. When presented with information, an idea, or a method, he asks this question: "Does it produce more resilience and good in the world?" His hope is that as you read this book you find yourself answering 'Yes' to what you find and realise.

He is also the author of *Life on Purpose - Your true calling and how to create it*. You can learn more at www.philipoudevrielink.com.

Preface

A problem worth answering

For many years I was frustrated with the multitude of books that described fulfilment and purpose without really answering how to arrive at an insight deep enough to be satisfyingly self-evident. Purpose and fulfilment was a very well described mystery that remained no less mysterious.

I like a problem worth answering and to address this mystery I developed a method and wrote a book that helps people derive a profound answer, not only understand the idea of answering.

A bigger problem worth answering

Over many years, I've had countless hundreds of conversations with people at all levels of organisations around workplace culture and culture change. Everyone admits that culture is critical for effective execution and success. Yet, usually only privately, the vast majority of people admit that culture and culture change remains a great mystery. Even those who 'specialise' in culture change admit, though always off-the-record, culture is poorly understood. In effect and despite an abundance of positive intention, something that's critical for success in any organisation largely remains a great unknown.

That's a problem worth answering.

Formalising an approach

Over the past few of years I've sought to address this problem worth answering. Culture involves customers, employees and stakeholders, and so too does the answer.

When the answer goes beyond description and instead is because of customers, employees and stakeholders, it's self-evident and relevant, embedded in the work and strategic. Employees are innately engaged, and customers are delighted — engaged with what they value and delighted with their valued experience.

This concise book outlines this approach to the work of culture and culture change — an approach of continuous culture regeneration using all the factors of cultural leadership and influence.

It is born of years of trial and error and the relentless pursuit and desire for practical completeness. It shows how to create business relevant and strategic culture — one that you must be more of to delight customers and engage employees to optimally support execution and achieve results.

Acknowledgements

I've been blessed to have involved and discussed my thinking and approach with many of you. For those of you I have worked with and who have been in this journey with me, I deeply appreciate what you've shared and the way you shared it.

To everyone that I have worked with: I am deeply blessed to have worked with you. You're a reminder that the wonderful thing about the work I do is that I get to work with such wonderful people.

Thank you to Andrew, Anthony, Ben, Clayton, Dion, Gareth, Jane, Jeff, Justine, Keri, Mandy, Matthew, Mark, Martin, Mary, Melanie, Nick, Richard, Rita, Robyn, Sally, Sasha, Shaheen, Steven, Suzannah, Tim, and Zaheed. You helped me identify assumptions and mysteries that I have now addressed, and to evolve a language that best helps clarify the topic and my approach. Creation is interactive, and you've helped me craft something worth sharing.

Special acknowledgement

Stand neither on the head nor in the shadow of others, but on their shoulders.

My ability to help lead, live and create what's important is informed by the work and efforts of many others — leaders and thought leaders in the area of leadership, organisational culture and change. I am grateful for their depth of ability to enable others to be more clear and effective. On behalf of those I support and serve, thank you.

I am particularly appreciative and thankful for the work of Edgar Schein — Society of Sloan Fellows Professor of Management Emeritus and a Professor Emeritus at the MIT Sloan School of Management. Edgar Schein is widely regarded and generally credited with inventing the term *corporate culture*.

The approach that I have developed for cultural leadership and change is consistent with, honours, and builds on his notable work in this field. He is the author of several books, namely *Organizational Culture and Leadership*, and *Corporate Culture Survival*

Guide. Both of these books underpin the approach to cultural leadership and change that this book describes, and are references.

Building on Edgar Schein's work

Schein's organisational culture model[1] is a three level hierarchy:

- **Artefacts.** The visible elements, including behaviour.
- **Espoused values.** Stated values and rules of behaviour.
- **Assumptions.** Shared, taken-for-granted, usually unconscious.

The model presented in this book (refer to page 30) uses several interrelated dimensions that cover and extend Schein's levels:

- **Strategy.** The tangible elements of what's experienced. This includes Schein's *artefacts* and *espoused values*. Those elements, including behaviour, language and what is espoused, is part of the overall strategy. I've moved Schein's *espoused values* into the eight cultural factors, part of the factor of *promotion* (refer to page 40).
- **Experience.** The experience of those tangible elements, including how espoused values are experienced. This is about actual values.
- **Culture.** The enduring shared meaning given to experience. This is equivalent to Schein's *assumptions*.

Adding the fourth level to Schein's model and how they fit with the dynamic culture model and eight factors of cultural leadership presented in this book, is shown here.

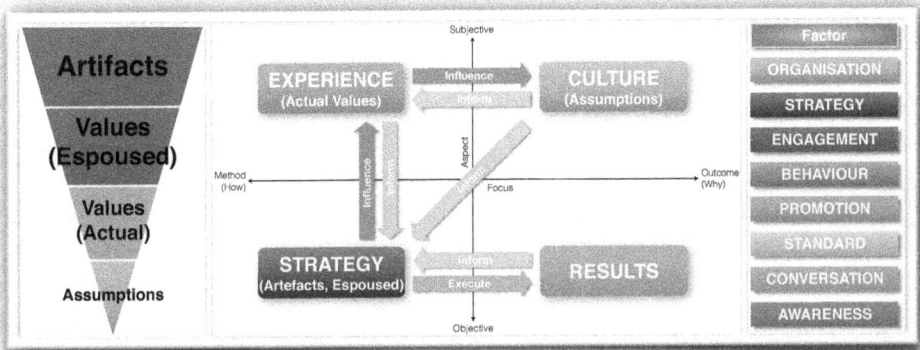

Adding to Schein's levels.   Overall dynamic model indicating Schein's levels.   Factors.

Generically specific

Edgar Schein describes two types of approach to culture and culture change: one that seeks to identify generic traits to be broadly applied to many organisations, though is removed from the here-and-now of organisational events and the decisions people face; and another that's embedded in the here-and-now and informs immediate situations and decisions.[3]

I have sought to create a general approach for identifying the specific — generically specific — a widely applicable approach to finding the nuances to look for and work with. This book introduces broad theoretical principles that any leader, manager, or organisation can apply to illuminate their local situations.

Alternate start to your reading

If you like to start your reading with examples of what happens when this work is applied, please read and familiarise yourself with the examples described on pages 33 - 35.

References

1. Schein, Edgar H.. Organizational Culture and Leadership. 4th ed. Hoboken: John Wiley & Sons, Inc., 2010. Kindle.
2. Schein, Edgar H.. Organizational culture and leadership. 2nd ed. San Francisco: Jossey-Bass, 1992. Print.
3. Schein, Edgar H.. The corporate culture survival guide. New and rev. ed. San Francisco, CA: Jossey-Bass, 2009. Kindle.
4. Schein, Edgar H.. "Corporate culture." Leadership and culture. MIT. Boston. Date unknown, 2005 approx.. Lecture. Citations provided by a colleague.
5. Crabtree, Steve. Gallup research. http://www.gallup.com/poll/165269/worldwide-employees-engaged-work.aspx. Accessed October 2013.
6. Kotter, John P.. Leading Change. 1st ed. Harvard Business Review Press, 2012. Kindle.

Why does culture matter?

Why is soft so hard?

An organisation exists because of people. When you have people together, culture exists.

A senior manager of a public company, initially proud of the new culture initiative they'd recently launched, admitted that she wasn't clear or confident that the approach they were taking was going to work. "We've done culture change this way before, trying to create what we think we should be, and it's never really worked. We know culture is critical, though there doesn't seem to be any alternative way."

There is an alternative. Rather than try to become what people suggest you should be, you can become what your own evidence shows you must be — strategic and relevant.

Culture matters because it significantly effects an organisation's long-term economic and service delivery performance. A culture that matters most is one that best supports the business strategy.

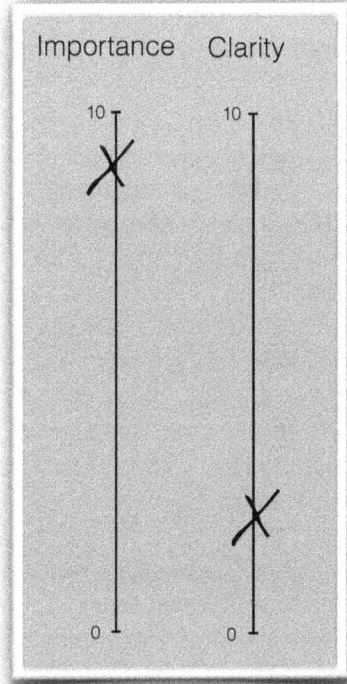

Culture is one of the most important and unclear aspects of organisational performance.

Performing culture?

You can have metrics that tell you your strategy and execution is good. Yet customers and employees can still say it isn't. For many, the way we're working is no longer working. But how do we change things?

Not understanding your culture means not understanding how it affects your employee engagement. Passionate employees is good for them and your results. Globally, according to Gallup[5] research, 13% of employees are engaged. In Australia and New Zealand, that figure is 24%. That's not just a problem of the lives of staff, but a problem of customer experience, productivity and results.

Not understanding your culture means not understanding how it affects the people your organisation serves (alternatively known as customers, clients, practise members, and service recipients). Delighting customers is good for them and your results.

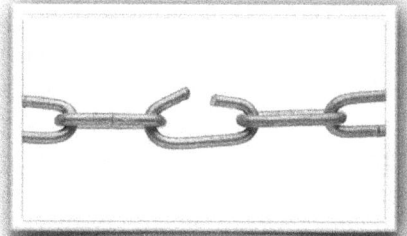

Business people at all levels of organisations all say that culture is critically important. They also admit that their level of clarity and confidence about how to influence culture, let alone creating one optimally aligned with the purpose of their organisation, is extremely low — a mystery.

Survive and thrive

Being out of sync is bad for business. Being out of tune with your internal and external environment — employees and clients — means you have a reduced ability to successfully adapt. Those who thrive have a complete ability to adapt — to positively adjust to external circumstance and to successfully integrate that internally.

Organisations with performance-centric, strategically aligned cultures experience better performance and growth. The question remains though — what makes a culture optimal and how do you create it?

What's wrong with culture change?

It's not change for change sake.

You might have tried, in the past, to work with and change your team or organisation's culture — with mixed success. Even with the of best intentions, investing time, effort and energy trying to shift that elusive, intangible 'thing' of culture often doesn't seem to change much. Resistance kicks in, inertia counteracts momentum, and things often end up looking a lot like they did before. Often the result is a little worse than before, though few would admit to that.

You might know that culture is important, be invested in the idea of culture change and transformation, yet somehow the approach you're taking and the advice you're receiving still doesn't seem to adequately explain why you're being asked to do certain things. You might want to know — is there a way to understand culture that explains how it's created and sustained and better informs how to influence it positively?

You might even have experienced huge culture change initiatives where, in the end, nothing really changed other than the sense that it might have been money better spent. You might be questioning — why is a given approach to culture change the way to go?

Sometimes, even with huge investment of time, money and resources, the conversation around culture and culture change still doesn't seem that relevant. You might be asking — how is culture strategically relevant?

There are often well-intentioned culture change initiatives designed to increase staff engagement. They might even be successful, with employees more engaged in the workplace. There's no doubt that engagement is important but it is not, by itself, the objective. Staff engaged towards the objective is. You might be reflecting — how to go beyond 'lovely' to 'actively supporting the strategy'?

Even when the importance of culture is understood, it's not widely known how culture supports execution and the achievement of results. It's almost as if there's two separate conversations — one about strategy and another about culture. We know they're related, though many don't exactly know how. You might be deliberating — how does culture translate to execution?

Out of a desire to understand culture and how to influence it well, you might have invested in reading, studying and attending training on the subject. Yet, the nature and dynamic of culture still remains a mystery. You might be curious about — what is culture anyway and is there a better way of understanding it?

Very often the usual approach to getting the tangible things done doesn't seem to be working when it comes to the intangibles. Sometimes it's making things worse. We know that the benefits of great culture are focus, motivation, engagement, connection, cohesion, resilience and a sense of spirit. Yet no matter how much we try, things often don't seem to be improving. You might be seeking — is there a better way?

You might be in an environment where you're invested in crafting your organisation's values and be a participant in regular 'cultural events', only for cultural survey results to show things really haven't changed. Pockets of flare-ups are dealt with, but it seems to keep happening. Despite your best efforts, your existing strategies somehow seem incomplete, with continuing frustration with a less than optimally productive culture. You might be asking — how can culture be intentionally influenced and successfully maintained?

You might even have the occasional individual who has influence beyond their role, who is widely respected and trusted as an example of fostering the kind of productive culture that many aspire to. Yet it seems difficult to reproduce on a wider scale — a scale we often sense, deep-down, is possible. You might be asking — how do we get more people to engage with and model the appropriate standard more often?

Due to a frequent lack of clarity, relevance and success with culture change you might have developed a kind of cynicism. You might acknowledge that 'culture' is important yet regard working with culture as irrelevant, still be frustrated with an apparent inability to work with 'it' successfully, or disappointed with those whose responsibility it was to do so.

These kinds of experience make perfect sense. Often we just don't know how to most effectively influence and shape our organisation's culture in a way that most productively supports the goals of the organisation. Edgar Schein reportedly agrees: "If you set out to change the culture, you end up in fog."[4]

Culture just seems hard to work on. Even for those with the greatest of intent, this confusion is usually due to misunderstanding the nature of culture, not realising the different stages that culture moves through as it ascends from chaos towards seamless transformation and renewal, and what the practise is for how to work with culture successfully.

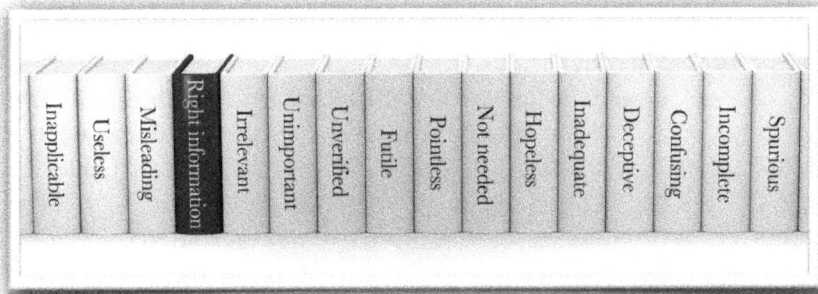

When it comes to culture, it's not always easy to know from which book we're reading...

A most tangible intangible?

Culture can help or hinder optimal performance - but what is it?

Culture or strategy?

There are many divergent arguments over whether culture or strategy is more significant, and whether it's true that "culture trumps strategy every time". Peter Drucker, the Austrian-born American management consultant who helped create the philosophical and practical foundations of the modern business corporation, reportedly said, "culture eats strategy for breakfast". In other words, ignore culture at your peril.

Few would argue that both great culture and effective strategy support greatest success. You can have great strategy, but a poor culture can lead to an inability to execute and a failure to deliver. You can have a great culture that still fails due to poor strategy or a competitors lesser culture with a better strategy. Many a great culture has disappeared due to poor strategy, and many a great strategy has been left undone due to poor culture. A great culture can revitalise a poor strategy, and an unproductive culture can doom even the best strategy.

The point is that great performance requires both effective strategy and productive culture. Strategy and culture work together. To be at your best requires the ability to understand, appreciate and integrate both the value of strategy and the nature of culture — not just separately, but also how they influence and shape each other.

So is culture or strategy more important? My experience suggests that strategy and culture are both important — equally important though in different and complimentary ways. In other words, since they're so closely interrelated, ignore culture or strategy at your peril.

In my view, **culture is strategy**. That's why I describe an optimally aligned culture as a strategic culture.

Seeing culture

Culture is all the invisible stuff that binds people in organisations together. Invisible and non-linear, culture is hard to control, evaluate, and manage. Even though we experience culture continuously, because it's invisible, it's usually unclear, ambiguous and difficult to interpret.

We see the objective, concrete manifestations of work performed — reports written, products delivered, sales secured, meetings held, clients served, processes followed, cost-for-profit, campaigns run, projects completed, and dividends per share.

What we don't see is the subjective side of how the work is performed — the feelings, perceptions, judgements, attitudes, meanings and values that define how the work and workplace is experienced. Culture cannot be treated as a tangible, finite object. ***Culture has to do with the invisible, subjective aspect of human experience.***

Intentional or accidental

It's often said that culture "is how things are done around here". Culture is therefore a primary factor that influences how people get things done. Culture influences execution which drives performance. No matter how brilliant your vision or strategy, neither will be realised if not supported by your culture.

For many managers though, culture's invisibility leads it to remain unaddressed and left to evolve unattended, accidentally and by chance. Since how things get done is what drives performance, this means that for many managers, the primary factor that determines performance is left to chance. When culture is left to chance, the engine that drives performance is left to chance. That's quite a gamble.

Leaving culture to evolve accidentally is high risk. Doing so intentionally takes effort — though the rewards are worth it. **Culture is always evolving — by accident or by design.**

Culture's noble intent

Groups of people have their own way of getting things done and their own way of talking about what it is doing and why it is doing so. But what caused that way of working to happen in the first place?

Edgar Schein[3] said that culture is "a pattern of shared basic assumptions that was learned by a group as it solved its problems of external adaptation and internal integration, that has worked well enough to be considered valid and, therefore, to be taught to new members as the correct way to perceive, think, and feel in relation to those problems."

What this means is that in response to challenge and circumstance, a group of people learns how to survive and grow, and in adapting successfully, what to communicate and how to behave. Methods that work, and do not, are taught to others as the right and wrong ways to work. Successful adaptation is another way of describing resilience. When culture functions optimally, the organisation functions resiliently.

Culture is both adaptive to external circumstance and distributes what is learned for internal cohesion. In other words, **culture is externally adaptive and internally integrative.**

This is the organisational version of what Charles Darwin wrote about in *Origin of Species* — that those who survive and thrive are the ones who most accurately perceive their environment and successfully adapt to that.

External adaptation is only truly complete when it is internally integrated.

Strategic culture

Strategy is about means to an end — achieving ends through mobilising means. Strategy is about creating the future. A brilliant strategy includes everything that's needed and only what's needed — including culture.

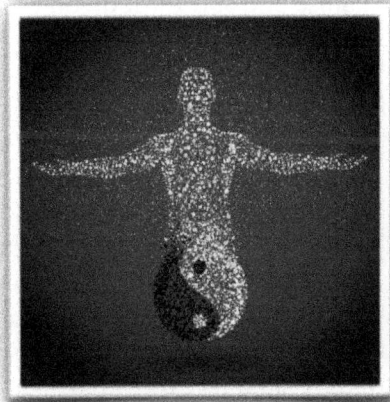

While **strategy is about the work, culture is about the experience.** Strategy describes how the work is to be done, and culture is the subjective human result of doing so.

Culture shapes strategy and is not strategy. Strategy shapes culture and is not culture. Culture humanises strategy.

Culture is both due to and determines people's experience of the strategy. We work to a strategy which we experience according to culture. That experience both reflects culture and directs the cultural trajectory.

Strategy and culture are different, shape each other, and both matter. Neglect either at your peril.

Influencing strategy

Culture and strategy interact and ideally mutually reinforce each other.

Culture is a complex set of variables that must be factored into the cluster of inputs that you consider, organise and sort through on the path to crafting your strategy.

The best strategy is determined using your productive culture as a filter — the criterion you use for the choices you make.

In this way, culture acts as a set of constraints or boundaries that ideally condition and determine other aspects of the strategy. The strategy choices themselves ideally reflect and strengthen the culture that most productively supports the strategy's objectives.

Whatever options are consistent with the productive culture is within the line, anything else is over the line. In other words, strategy simultaneously aims to achieve the desired results and craft the culture that best supports its achievement.

Strategy is about elimination — elimination of the choices that do not support execution. ***Culture is a necessary criteria for your strategic choices.***

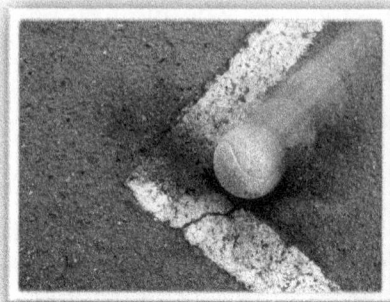

Business of experience

Culture is shaped from how the work and workplace is experienced. People — customers and employees — feel valued when they experience their values.

Culture matters for employees. People join your company on the promise, though leave due to their experience. They remain engaged in work when they experience their values at work and in the workplace. In this way, culture is an integral aspect of attracting and retaining talent.

Culture matters for customers. Though people may buy your company's product or service, they remain loyal, recommend or condemn, due to their experience. Customers feel valued when they experience their values — whenever and however they interact with your business. Every time a customer experiences a touch-point with your organisation, they experience that according to their values — either their presence or absence. In this way, culture is an integral aspect of attracting and delighting customers.

It pays to know and to deliver what your customers and employees value as their experience. They'll tell you anyway — they'll complain about what they value and aren't getting if they don't. In this way, *culture can be a highly reliable way for delivering high value customer experience and employee engagement.* By leaving culture to chance you're leaving the delivery of the valued experience of staff and customers to chance.

Culture renews strategy

Every organisation needs talented strategic thinkers, business leaders, and effective leadership development and succession. Renewal in these areas is needed for any organisation to sustain and revitalise productivity, execution and competitiveness. This renewal is only possible in a culture that values it.

This aspect of culture — supporting and directing the renewal of business, leadership and strategic capability — only happens when the culture values, demands and drives these capabilities.

Culture continually seeks to regenerate what it considers strategically important, even when it's not aware that it is doing so.

Experiencing culture

Culture is created by people. People interact socially through improvised and unscripted communication. It is through this communication system, in particular the use of language, that cultural values are created, reinforced and changed. *Language reflects and directs culture.*

We don't see someone else's subjective experience and values. We see the objective manifestation of them. In response we have our own subjective experience and the presence or compromise of our values.

We subjectively experience the visible, objective aspects of others — their personality, character traits, and the healthy and unhealthy expression of their values — according to our values which we individually interpret and give meaning to. That becomes 'my' experience.

Likewise, we subjectively experience and interpret the objective aspects of the work and workplace — the structures, systems, processes, behaviours and expressions — according to our values which we collectively interpret and give meaning to. That shapes 'our' experience.

Conversations with culture

We live and perceive through our values — albeit their healthy or unhealthy expression. In other words, we perceive our environment — systems, structures and behaviours — according to the presence or absence of our values and interpret meaning accordingly. We usually do this according to our habits of meaning making.

When we do this as a group — influencing, confirming, refuting and shaping meaning — we create shared assumptions and culture. Individually we confirm our own meaning. Collectively we confirm meaning with each other through conversation. *Our conversation and language reflects, directs and shapes culture.*

Outsourcing culture?

Every organisation has a culture. That culture is continuously being created. Unfortunately, many, if not most, cultures develop invisibly and unintentionally. That culture is invisible, does not mean that it does not exist.

Culture is often understood as a 'people' aspect of business that people assume therefore belongs to and is delegated to HR. Though intangible, responsibility for culture is far too important to be delegated — it's one of the most important drivers of success for you, your teams, and your organisation. As such, *culture is a leadership responsibility.*

Edgar Schein agrees that: "the only thing of real importance that leaders do is to create and manage culture."[2] He is clear about the need to work with culture intentionally when he says, "If you do not manage culture, it will manage you—and you may not even be aware of the extent to which this is happening."[3] Culture change is intentional. This concurs with one definition of leadership I often use which is that *leadership is constant adaptation with intention.*

Enduring, sustainable success is dependent on a culture that productively supports your strategy. Culture is the result of how people in your organisation experience and make meaning about how the work gets done. Though some people, e.g. those in senior positions, clearly have more influence than others, the culture that's created is a product of everyone's ongoing contribution — though especially the influence of the person in charge.

Culture is continually informing how people function and interpret their experience, and that shared interpretation is continually influencing and shaping culture. Everyone participates and influences — some intentionally, most inadvertently. Even those who think they aren't influencing culture are still influencing it because of how they participate with it.

Culture is therefore everyone's responsibility — everyone's leadership responsibility.

Learning to influence and shape culture can be delegated. Responsibility for influencing and shaping culture, cannot. You wouldn't outsource leadership — so don't outsource culture.

Multi or unitary?

With all the frequent talk about 'organisational culture', it's easy to think that this means that there's a "single organisational culture".

Besides a single culture, an organisation can also be understood as being made up of multiple subcultures that can, and very often do, vary greatly from each other. These subcultures coexist in different ways — in harmony, indifference or conflict — and support the organisation's strategy to varying degrees.

Groups have culture, and subgroups have subculture. Subcultures all have as their reference the organisation's values, though each subculture brings them to life in their own distinct ways, and adds to them according to what's valued by the people living it.

An organisation's culture and its subcultures coexist.

Who sets the standards?

We all know that a fish swims head first. Like culture, it's also true that it is unlikely to be aware of the water it's swimming in.

There's also an old saying that a fish rots from the head down — meaning that an organisation's culture and group's subculture originate and are influenced most powerfully by the person with greatest influence — usually the person in charge.

The way the leader behaves, communicates, what they act on and what is left behind, the standard they address and the one they let go, what is rewarded and what is punished, what they pay attention to and ignore, what they show is important and irrelevant — all collectively form a potent and continuous signature that influences the experience and collective meaning-making of the people in that group — demonstrating and modelling a de facto standard. *The leaders example sets the standard — others interpretation of their example becomes the standard.*

A productive culture is one that optimally supports the strategy and achievement of its purpose. The leader's example powerfully sets a de facto standard. What matters is that what they model is aligned with the productive culture that best helps achieve the intended results.

What do you work on?

It's not possible to work on outcomes directly — only to work on what produces them.

When they're not satisfied with the results they're getting, many people immediately set out to change their results. The problem is that outcomes cannot be worked on directly. To set out to change your results, you end up in fog. If you set out to change your methods — your strategy for achieving your results — you achieve different results.

Edgar Schein reportedly said "if you set out to change the culture, you end up in fog. If you set out to change behaviours, then you'll change the culture."[4] This means that **culture is an outcome.**

To change culture, behaviours and more importantly, the meanings associated with them, needs to change.

The point is that **to change the culture, you need to change the factors and methods — your strategy — that produces it.**

Continuously discontinuous

Many think that culture change is a finite program — like any other project with a start and a finish. Some expect the culture to be different when the culture change project is complete.

Others think of culture as a single event or series of functions in the workplace — each of which have a beginning and an end. Branded as 'culture change events', many experience them as disconnected from the work and their general experience of the workplace.

People in an organisation or group are continuously experiencing what happens, influencing each other, having conversations, and shaping the meaning they give to what happens. This happens continuously. Part of what happens in the workplace are projects and events. The way people experience those projects and events is a separate thing entirely.

A product of meaning-making based on how the work and the workplace is continuously experienced, *culture is developed continuously.*

Continuously being influenced and additive, culture is always becoming — becoming more of — something. What matters is whether that something optimally supports your strategy. *Culture is always becoming 'more of'.*

Effective change projects are important. Workplace events that engage are important. However, neither of them are a substitute for intentional and successful culture change. Culture happens continuously. Since culture is being continuously created, influenced and recreated — so *culture change must be and is continuous.*

Why does culture seem so complex?

Humans are complex. Culture is human. Culture is therefore complex. It seems complex because, well, it is. That doesn't mean your approach to culture can't be elegant — indeed it can be. It's a mistake to try to make it simplistic.

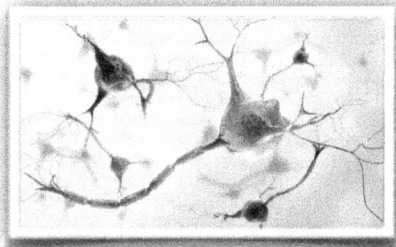

Culture's complexity is demonstrated and influenced through all the many factors that influence human experience and the way people together make meaning. Those factors are sometimes simple, often complicated and invariably complex — including what's addressed, funded, focussed on, recognised, rewarded, and reinforced.

Culture is complex and requires a complete and elegant approach to change it.

Planning for culture

Strategy is important. Action and execution is sequential. Most organisations place much importance on developing and having an integrated strategic plan. They invest heavily in its creation, and many of their employees participate in training on how best to produce and execute on them. For many organisations, their integrated strategic planning process is a huge investment in time, money, energy and resources.

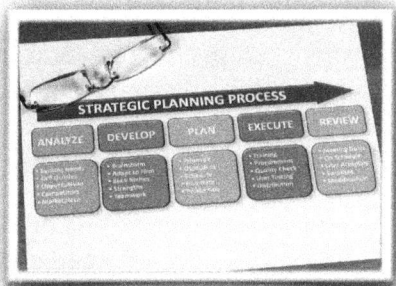

Culture is important. Culture and influence is continuous. ***Does your organisation have an integrated continuous culture plan? Do you know how to execute on that plan skilfully?***

Best strategy for the future?

Beyond the customer to valued experience

Continuing context

In general and including the context in which business has been successful, we've been through the Agricultural Age (farmers), Industrial Age (factory workers), and Information Age (knowledge workers). Some would argue we've recently moved into the consumer age.

Along with those broader ages, I see the historical perspective as the different approaches that business has taken to be successful — both for what they focus on during that age, the limitation of the previous age they solved, and what they added to the previous age to do so.

Providing for clients and customers

We've lived through and still utilise what each age has contributed towards business success, and in the process we've moved from a completely tangible age to increasingly subjective ones:

Agricultural Age	Farmers producing resources for local market
Industrial Age	Factory workers manufacturing for local market
Production Age	Factory workers mass producing to scale for a wider market
Distribution Age	Transport workers using connections to reach a global market
Information Age	Office workers using connected networks to access controlled data
Customer Age	Buyers accessing goods and services according to their preferences
Experience Age	People preferring to perceive they've received their valued experience

Unless they're a monopoly, organisations are failing when they aren't providing access to and delivering according to customer preferences. The organisations that are thriving are the ones that understand perception and deliver valued experience — for both customers and staff.

Today's business landscape is beyond customer preferences and customer experience alone. This is because of the emerging realisation that when it comes to valued experience — people experience their interactions according to their own values —

people feel valued when they experience their own values.

Integration matters because you can only externally deliver experience you internally bring to life.

More than be the change, it's be the valued experience.

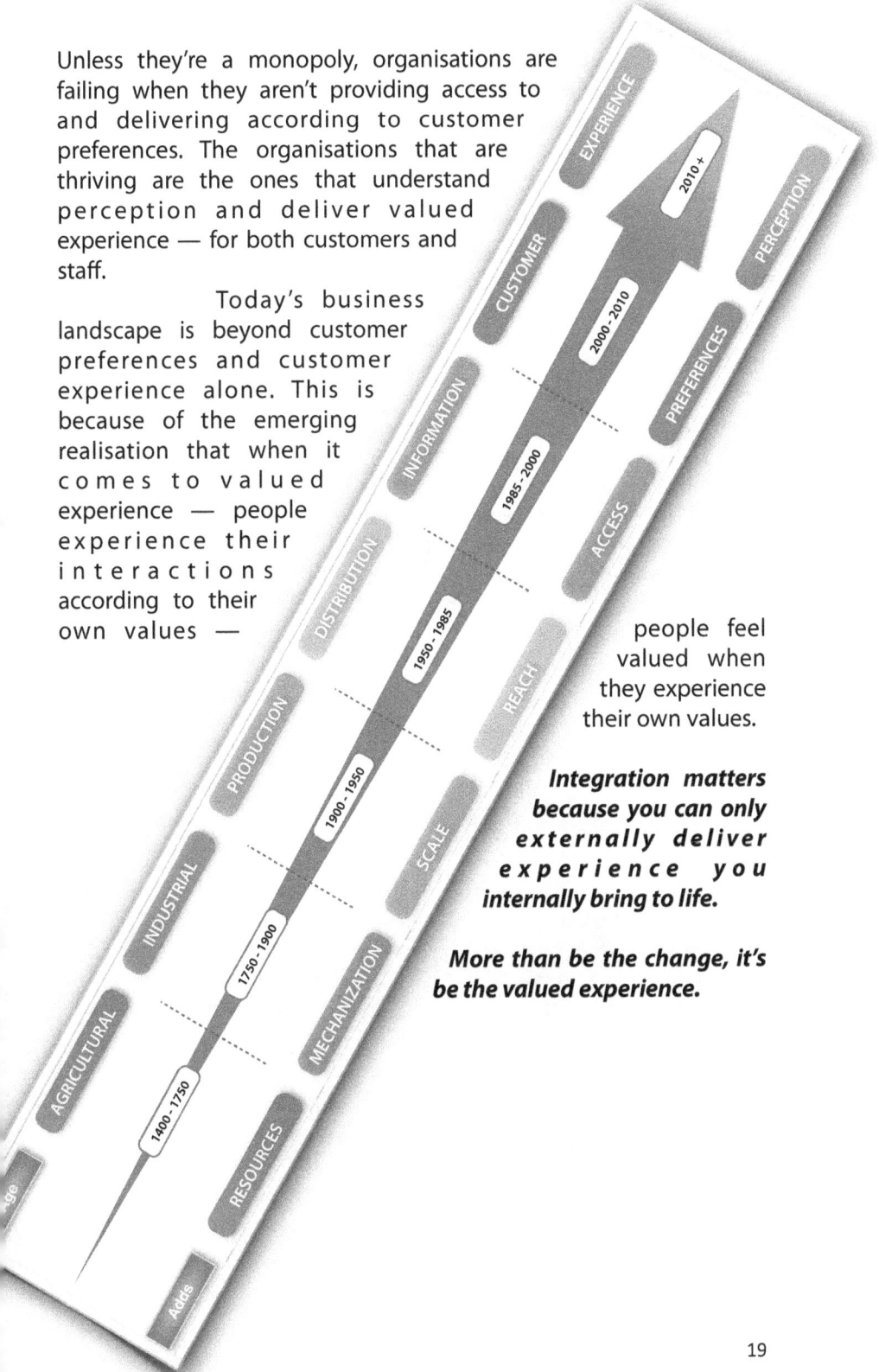

EXPERIENCE

PERCEPTION

CUSTOMER

PREFERENCES

INFORMATION

ACCESS

DISTRIBUTION

REACH

PRODUCTION

SCALE

INDUSTRIAL

MECHANIZATION

AGRICULTURAL

RESOURCES

2010+

2000-2010

1985-2000

1950-1985

1900-1950

1750-1900

1400-1750

Adds

...ge

How does culture evolve and mature?

From chaotic stagnation to seamless transformation

We've found that culture, and approaches to culture, progress through identifiable stages. Each successive stage includes elements of the stages before it — so is an evolutionary model. Most organisations have elements of multiple stages. What matters is where the culture and approach to culture is centred and how well it integrates the stages prior.

The following stages of cultural maturity model shows the progressive shift in approach to culture and charts the various maturity stages that culture can move through. Each successive stage contributes more to the business objective and strategy.

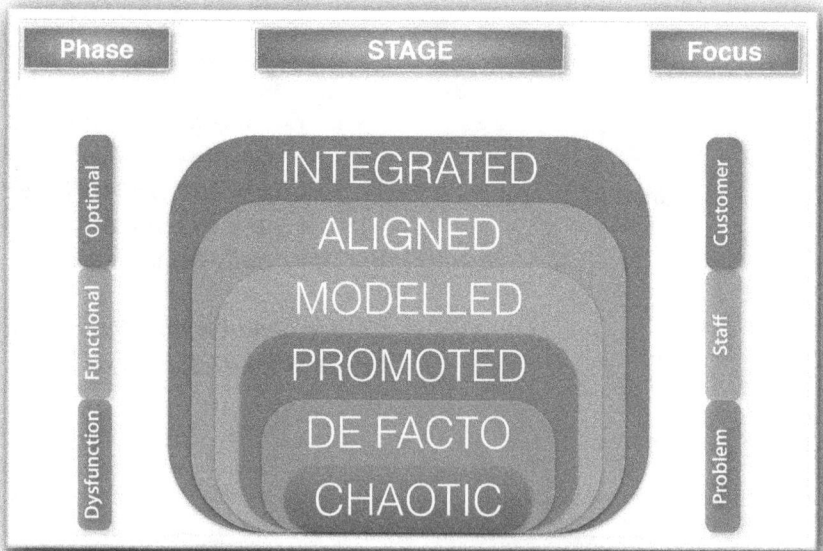

Phase	STAGE	Focus
Optimal	INTEGRATED	Customer
Functional	ALIGNED	Staff
	MODELLED	
Dysfunction	PROMOTED	Problem
	DE FACTO	
	CHAOTIC	

The evolutionary Stages of Culture Maturity and the progressive approaches to culture change.

STAGE 1: Chaotic

The most unaware stage is chaotic, uncontrolled, reactive, impulsive — it's a problem that persists unabated. Usually disruptive, some would call this dysfunctional, perhaps 'toxic'. In all likelihood, the culture is actively unproductive and staff are actively disengaged.

There tends to be a lack of awareness about how culture is affecting and inhibiting business, engagement and productivity. Many may even regard these problematic aspects of culture as 'normal' and therefore not needing attention.

At this stage, the disruptive and unproductive nature of culture remains unaddressed. The usual standard is 'anything goes'. Whatever the culture is, it's unlikely to contribute anything, if at all, to the execution of strategy and achievement of results.

Phase	STAGE	Focus
Dysfunction	CHAOTIC	Problem

Stage 1: The chaotic first stage of problematic dysfunction.

STAGE 2: De Facto

At the chaotic stage, problematic situations remain unaddressed, and there's an 'anything goes' standard. At the de facto stage, a standard exists, though it is created by default through what people model and uphold.

The way the most influential people behave, communicate, act on, leave behind, address, ignore, reward, punish, pay attention to, indicate is important and irrelevant — all continuously demonstrate, model and reinforce a standard. By default, it influences and eventually becomes the accepted standard — the de facto standard.

It's the standard that is demonstrated and dealt with. It's often confusing and unclear, as people infer, interpret and pass on behaviours, regardless of the values they represent.

At its worst, aspects of the chaotic culture are addressed, though interventions are usually inconsistently applied and even then by the motivated minority. As the standard is largely based on the enacted standards of the most influential, it can seem like people are walking on eggshells. Programs and specific interventions are often implemented to tactically address specific behavioural issues in different areas of the organisation — usually with mixed success due to inconsistent application.

There's awareness that the actively unproductive and inhibiting aspects of culture need to be dealt with — particularly when significantly disruptive — usually with the aim of reliably and consistently minimising any ongoing disruption.

However, even though the unhelpful aspects of culture are addressed, there tends to be a lack of awareness about what is fuelling and sustaining them. This stage can seem like you're putting out fires without ever truly understanding what's igniting them, or upon what basis to consistently approach them.

At its best, the de facto culture is alive and well, and is according to what's expedient for the most influential people in the organisation or group. It's not defined — it reflects the standard at which the most influential are motivated to act consistently.

Stage 2: The usually inconsistent, de facto product of unintentional influence.

STAGE 3: Promoted

The promoted stage addresses the lack of consistency and direction of the de facto stage. It does this through acknowledging that a preferred aspiration is important for everyone in the organisation — that standards are important.

Certain values and culture are desired — at least in word. In the attempt to see them modelled in deed, the values and defined culture are actively espoused and promoted.

Well-meaning effort is made to identify what would be regarded as a helpful and functional cultural aspiration for staff. Very often research is accessed, diagnostics are used, courses are attended and books are read — all with the aim to form and define the ideal culture. The espoused values and preferred culture are written down, published and promoted.

Just as a strategic plan without action usually fails to produce the intended results, the cultural challenge at this stage is largely the same — one of execution. The challenge at this stage is that a statement of intent does not yet bring values to life and automatically produce momentum that's able to create a living, vibrant culture that's aligned with what's being promoted.

Culture is recognised as another aspect of the organisation that is to be managed. With the aspirational cultural traits identified, some effort and thought is put towards programs intended to support and reinforce those traits. The cultural initiative is usually

Phase	STAGE	Focus
Functional	PROMOTED	Staff
Dysfunction	DE FACTO	Problem
	CHAOTIC	

Stage 3: Focus on promoting a functional, staff-oriented culture.

viewed as any other form of project, with objectives, targets, activities and metrics. Like other strategic projects, delegated to a project group — sometimes a 'culture committee'.

Unfortunately, that group often tends to be made responsible and held accountable for the whole organisation's culture — something it can never achieve on its own. The group has neither the positional authority nor the ability to continuously influence the work and workplace to successfully shape the desired culture.

Due to the lack of appreciation for the nature of alignment and lack of clarity for how to influence and grow a productive culture that supports strategy, this stage is often characterised by participation in event-based initiatives. Though well intended, they are sometimes referred to as 'cultural events' or social 'happiness events' that aren't always fully aligned with the cultural aspiration or connected with the work and the workplace.

There's no doubt that effective workplace relationships are important, and these events can play an important role in supporting people to get to know each other — to feel personally connected. However, culture is fundamentally embedded in and about how the ongoing work and workplace is experienced, including before and after these events. Culture is far more than any series of events.

These events, while personally helpful from a social interaction perspective, are only one part of the experience of the work and workplace. The overall approach to culture is still misaligned from the goal of crafting a culture that most productively supports the strategic objectives. Culture is more than what people do — it's based on how people experience and make sense of what gets done and how it's done.

Usually interpreted as a whole-of-organisation standard, the defined standard isn't yet widely modelled in the workplace. While generally appreciated as a noble idea, staff are generally not widely engaged with the practise of bringing it alive. Very often, the source of the idealised cultural definition is external and people intuitively sense that it is unrelated to the work and the workplace that it's applied to.

At best, engagement with the espoused standard is limited and not distributed throughout the organisation. There are however, usually a few who do decide to model the espoused values and aspired culture. Where the gap between the old de facto standard and the desired standard remains, there's a risk for the first few who model that new standard. From the perspective of the prevailing culture, people who model the desired culture are regarded as outliers — negative outliers. Where the old standard is strong and reinforced, the people still living the previous culture may punish and in some cases expel these apparently negative outliers. Though they're in reality positive outliers — they become targets of the organisational immune system.

Others who experience them as positively aligned examples — positive outliers — will sometimes refer to them as cultural 'heroes'. The first to follow is paradoxically showing great leadership, and their leadership as positive outliers needs to be recognised, supported, promoted and rewarded — else the organisational immune systems take effect.

Moreover, at this stage the relationship between strategy and culture is often unrecognised or misunderstood, and the need for strategic alignment is either not realised or not fully appreciated. As such there's usually still a significant misalignment between strategy and cultural aspiration.

STAGE 4: Modelled

Many organisations have individuals, who could be at any level within the business, who proactively show up aligned with the aspired culture. They're proactive in assuming personal responsibility for ensuring they conduct themselves in a manner that's aligned with, reflects and directs what the organisation says matters.

The modelled stage exists when enough people — though not necessarily everyone — are actively referring to and modelling the promoted standard. It happens continuously and frequently enough for the de facto standard to become the promoted standard — they're aligned. The now aligned and promoted standard is seen as a base standard, the minimum to be upheld, the foundation on which to build.

By accident or by design, they've figured out how to behave according to their own personal values in a way that supports the desired organisational culture. As such, they're an example of the positive aspects of the productive culture. Not always initially appreciated, they're an example that others pay attention to, are influenced by, learn from and follow.

These people know that the standard they act on is the standard they set, and the standard they let go is the standard they sanction. Regardless of their position, they're leaders in their organisation.

People's focus on how behaviour is experienced is crucial. Edgar Schein, who reportedly said we end up in fog if we try to change culture directly, added, "If you set out to change behaviours, then you change the culture."[4] However, it's not just about behaviours — it's about how the behaviours are experienced.

Changing behaviour is usually the easiest way to influence and change people's experience. Being flexible, behaviour and especially language is usually the easiest to change compared to the other more fixed elements of structures and systems.

This stage exists when behaviour is consistently applied, consistently across the organisation, in a way that reinforces the experience that shapes the defined culture.

Rather than a single person influencing on their own, it's now multiple people influencing together. Consistent application is experienced as confirming the desired culture. This has a significant reinforcing effect. We can hear a message once, though when we receive it multiple times from multiple different sources, we 'get the message'. Multiple people regularly conveying the same experience effectively amplifies and embeds the message.

There's consistent and continuous alignment between personal action, message and meaning of the experience conveyed, and desired culture.

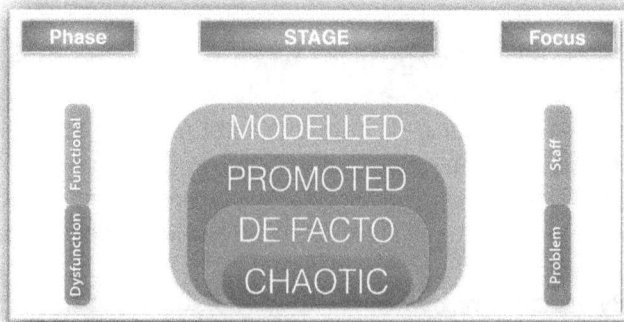

Phase	STAGE	Focus
Functional / Dysfunction	MODELLED / PROMOTED / DE FACTO / CHAOTIC	Staff / Problem

Stage 4: The desired staff-oriented functional culture is widely modelled.

The focus at this stage is on what a functional culture may be for staff. However, no matter how functional that culture may be, there's a risk that it is not yet optimally aligned towards the customer and therefore might not be most effectively supporting the strategy and purpose of the organisation.

STAGE 5: Aligned

The previous stage has distributed engagement of people behaving in a way that's aligned with the defined and functional staff-oriented culture.

Though it's reliably and consistently delivering valued experience for staff, it is not necessarily aligned with and delivering valued experience for customers. If customers are delighted through valued experience, then that's usually more by accident than by design.

In the aligned stage, people realise and appreciate that what's brought to life is what's experienced — by both employees and customers. Here, it's important that people live and model a functional culture that engages staff in a way that engages and is aligned towards delighting the customer.

When staff experience their values, they feel valued. When customers experience their values, they feel valued. This stage adds to the previous stage by adding the valued customer experience to

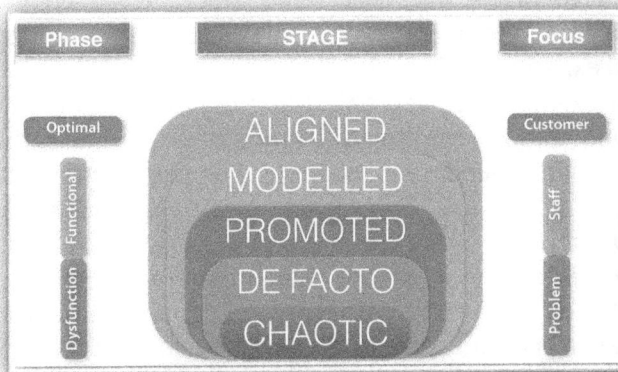

Stage 5: The modelled culture is optimally aligned towards the client and customer.

the valued staff experience — so that the organisation brings both to life. In that way, employees are engaged and customers are delighted.

This is as true for the organisation as a whole as it is for groups — subcultures — within the organisation.

For example, staff may value trust and collaboration, and customers value ease and timeliness. The combined definition is therefore collaboration, ease, timeliness and trust. By bringing all of those values to life means that staff are engaged and valued, as are the group's customers.

This combined standard becomes the enhanced standard for the promoted and modelled stages. Nothing is lost, though important valued experiences are added.

STAGE 6: Integrated

Once the flexible, behavioural aspects of the work and workplace are aligned and applied consistently enough, awareness usually turns towards the other elements of the work and workplace — the fixed elements of structure and systems — and whether they are experienced as consistent with the optimal culture, or not.

There tends to be a growing awareness that though aligned behaviour is important, the productive culture will always be less than optimal as long as the systems and structures remain unaligned and fragmented in terms of whether they support both the strategy and valued experience.

For example, you can have the most trustworthy colleagues in the world that create the experience of trust, but if the work design continually sends the message that you're untrusted, then there are opposing experiences and messages, and a less then optimal culture.

For example, it would be understandable if people experienced as untrusting, disrespectful, and disempowering a system that checks, rechecks and checks again people's work. The characteristic of the system is such that people don't experience trust, and receive the message of distrust. If trust is an important aspect of the productive culture, then the experience of the people working to that system is misaligned, and the ability to create a trusting culture is less than optimal, and therefore, less likely.

Along with ensuring consistent application of behaviour, this stage seeks to align all elements of the work and workplace, optimising the ability for their culture to sustainably be at its most productive.

It might be tempting to think that an integrated culture is complete and finished in an optimal way. However, it still takes vigilance to become aware of areas of misalignment and effort to reintegrate them. Eventually, integrating the productive culture not only becomes the way things are done, it becomes the demanded expectation that it continually renew itself that way.

There's awareness of any actual or possible deviation to the productive culture and immediate corrective action takes place. There's active motivation to become aware of and find opportunities to continually enrich and enliven the productive culture. In these ways, the culture transforms, renews and regenerates the work and workplace in a continually more productive manner.

Realignment and regeneration at this stage is a given — with the culture continually generating its own seamless transformation.

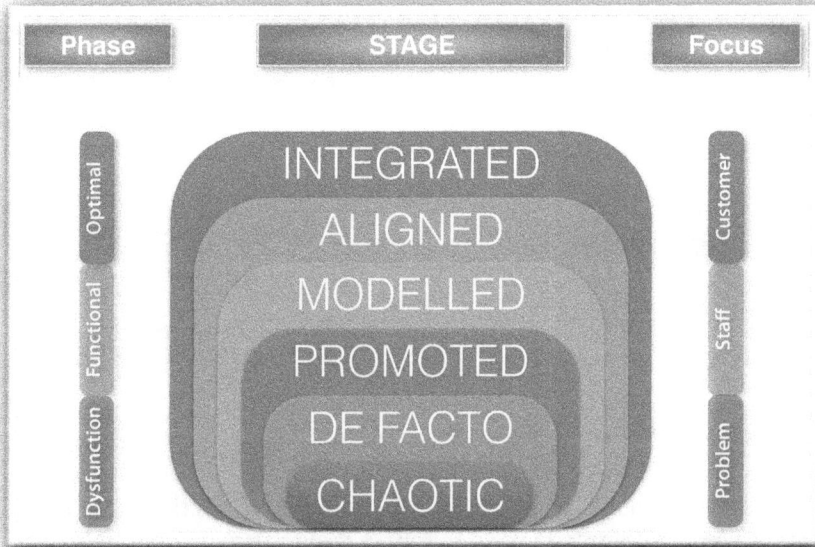

Phase	STAGE	Focus
Optimal	INTEGRATED	Customer
	ALIGNED	
Functional	MODELLED	Staff
	PROMOTED	
Dysfunction	DE FACTO	Problem
	CHAOTIC	

Stage 6: Systems integrated in supporting the optimal combined definition. The progressive Stages of Culture Maturity and approach to culture change are inclusive and evolutionary.

What dynamic drives culture?

Before setting out to influence and shape culture...

Strategy is all about how — the structures, systems, processes, behaviours and language through which the work is done. The way the work and workplace is experienced is influenced by the strategy in its totality, including the example set by the most influential.

Strategy is objective and the experience of strategy is its subjective aspect. As both strategy and experience relate to how, they're related to a focus on method. The execution of strategy leads to results. The shaping, reflection and direction of shared meaning derived from experience leads to culture. Both results and culture are outcomes — outcomes of the methods that produced them.

This is shown in the following culture dynamics model.

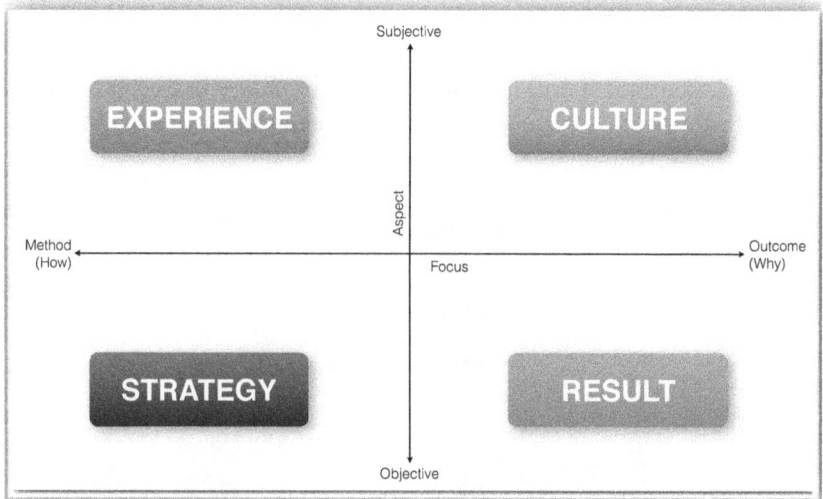

Outline of the quadrants and dimensions of the Strategic Culture Dynamics Model™

We can think of management as being about things, and leadership as being about people. Things and objects don't have subjective experience and cannot follow. People do have subjective experience and can follow. People choose to follow due to their experience.

Strategy, execution and results are all finite 'things' that are managed. Influencing people's experience and shaping culture are continuous acts of leadership. The difference between management and leadership can be defined as the boundary between objective things and subjective experience — which is all about influence. Management is finite, leadership is infinite.

This is represented in the following model, which adds to the previous outline of the Strategic Culture Dynamics Model™, and shows the management and leadership domains.

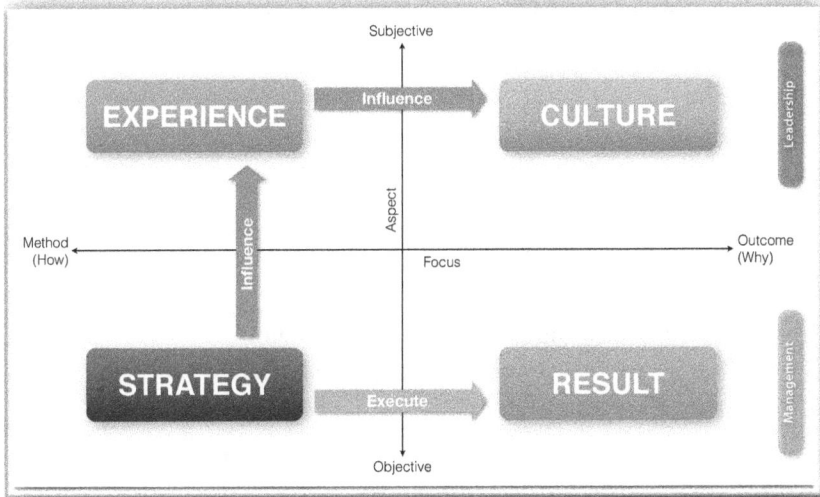

Strategic Culture Dynamics Model™ - how culture is influenced and shaped.

Strategy in its totality — structure, systems, processes, behaviours, language, the work, the work-design, and the workplace — is simultaneously the basis for achieving results and for influencing and shaping of the shared experience and meaning making that creates and sustains culture.

In the usual organisational context, the desired results inform the strategy needed to achieve them. Since strategy subsumes culture — uses culture as a selection and elimination filter for choices and decision making — the ideal strategy is informed by both results and the productive culture that best supports the organisation's ability to achieve those results. Moreover, the best strategy is informed by and adapts to the experience it influences.

This is represented in the following model, which adds to the previous outline and shows only that the different factors inform strategy. It also represents how the assumptions of culture are always informing, usually unconsciously, strategic choices.

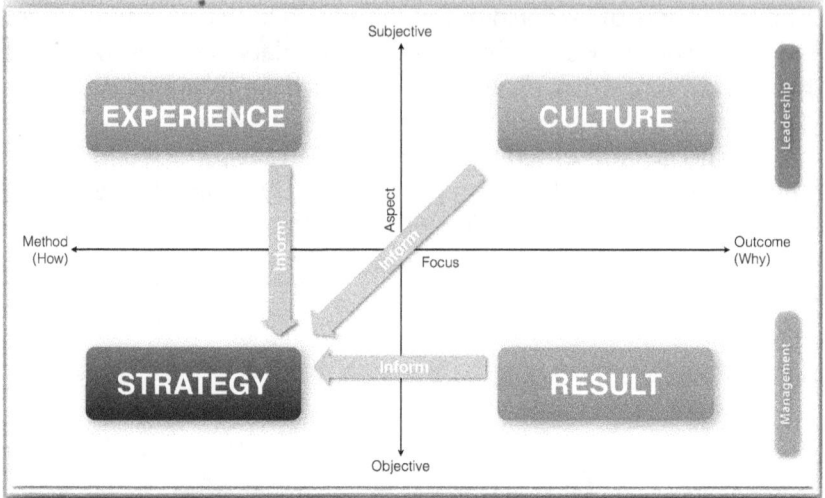

Strategic Culture Dynamics Model™ - strategy is informed by the culture it helps to create.

Fact is, culture also informs the way the work and workplace is experienced, and results inform and influence experience. The overall model is represented in the following diagram.

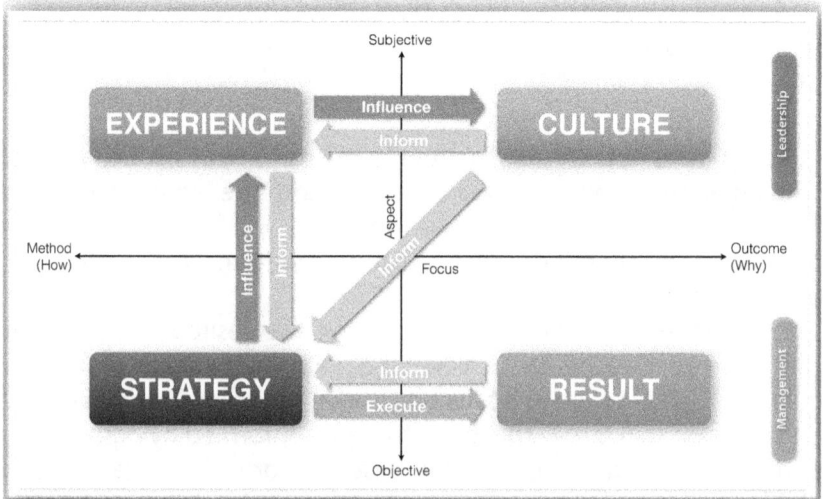

The overall Strategic Culture Dynamics Model™

Engaged alignment?

Each one of us has defining values, which when we act through and are in alignment with them, are the source of our greatest meaning and fulfilment.

Personal engagement is a necessary condition for group engagement.

When your personal values are integrated with others in your team into your group values, you have the innate source of greatest engagement for you and your team. The effective expression of your defining values contributes towards and supports team values and engagement. People are individually engaged towards group engagement.

Team engagement is a necessary condition for customer engagement. The effective expression of team values supports the delivery of valued customer experience.

Individual values fulfilment supports team engagement which supports customer delight.

The more that staff are engaged and customers are delighted, the more likely that stakeholders and shareholders will be satisfied.

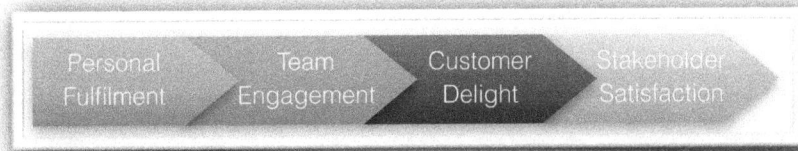

| Personal Fulfilment | Team Engagement | Customer Delight | Stakeholder Satisfaction |

The different and connected levels of engagement are virtuously supportive.

For example, a senior manager's fulfilment through empowering others actively supports the direction and trust that his leadership team innately engage through. In their situation, direction and trust naturally support and are necessary — in their words, critical — for the ease, clarity and competence their customers value and want to experience when interacting with them.

If we make it personal?

Consider again your closest personal relationship for a moment — say your life partner. The status label to describe that situation — let's call that 'married' — is the objective visible outcome you're in.

Most people would say they'd want their relationship to be one of happiness and joy. If the outcome you want is happiness and joy, then what does the overall method need to be to create it?

Well, each person's overall experience of the others will need to be happy and joyful if the outcome is to be characterised as happiness and joy. In other words, the way each person brings themselves to that relationship, the way they behave, express and talk — their strategy — will need to be experienced overall as happy and joyful by the others in that relationship.

If others in your relationship are not experiencing your strategy as happy and joyful — say as unhappy and sad — then you might want to be informed of that so you can change your joint strategy, or establish a change in mutual meaning associated with the joint strategy you're both using, so that it is.

The chosen strategy needs to influence the desired experience for the result to be the desired kind of relationship. If your strategy isn't being experienced as it needs to be, then you might want to think about changing your strategy or your agreed meaning.

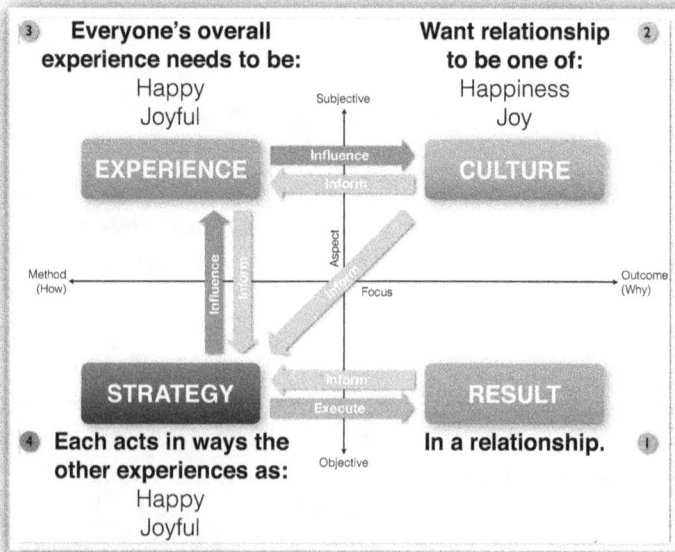

A real-world example (based on actual events)

From valued experience to strategic input

Valued experience I worked with

As the first part of their strategic planning offsite, a senior team in a major financial institution decided to clarify and define their strategic culture. Through a diagnostic process that looked at how they were currently being experienced, they understood that their customers were wanting to experience them as clear, honest, relational, responsible, and as partners — the experience they needed to create.

They also discerned that to be most engaged with their work, they themselves needed to experience their own team as collaborative, helpful and trusting — their innate values as a team.

They realised too that their values of collaboration, helpfulness and trust were critical for ensuring and essential to the delivery of the valued experience of their customers.

Cultural aspiration

The team distilled the valued experience of themselves and their customers into a value statement of clarity, helpfulness, interrelatedness, responsibility, and trust — a cultural aspiration which they described as a "trusted advisor" culture.

Their aspirational culture is not an externally imposed definition — it is a self-evident definition they all clearly saw was embedded in themselves and was a direct result of their work. In their words, "Not separate from, but completely relevant to our team, our work and our customers."

By understanding and combining the nature of their work, the people involved in delivering results, and the valued experience of their customers, they defined a cultural aspiration embedded in and relevant to their work. They realised that they had a definition which, when brought to life, would intrinsically engage them and delight their customers.

Strategic implications

Clear on the self-evident culture that they must become more of to engage themselves and delight their customers, they were able to immediately grasp the strategic implications.

Several loudly uttered expletives revealed that they'd realised that much of their current strategy was not only misaligned, but back to front. They needed to change that to become 'more of'.

The reason for using their cultural aspiration as their strategic assessment criteria was also clear for them. They did not resist their cultural definition — few people resist their own insights — and were naturally and actively engaged in applying it to their strategic planning and decision making. As the most senior manager shared, "This is who we must become more of."

This is represented in the following diagram.

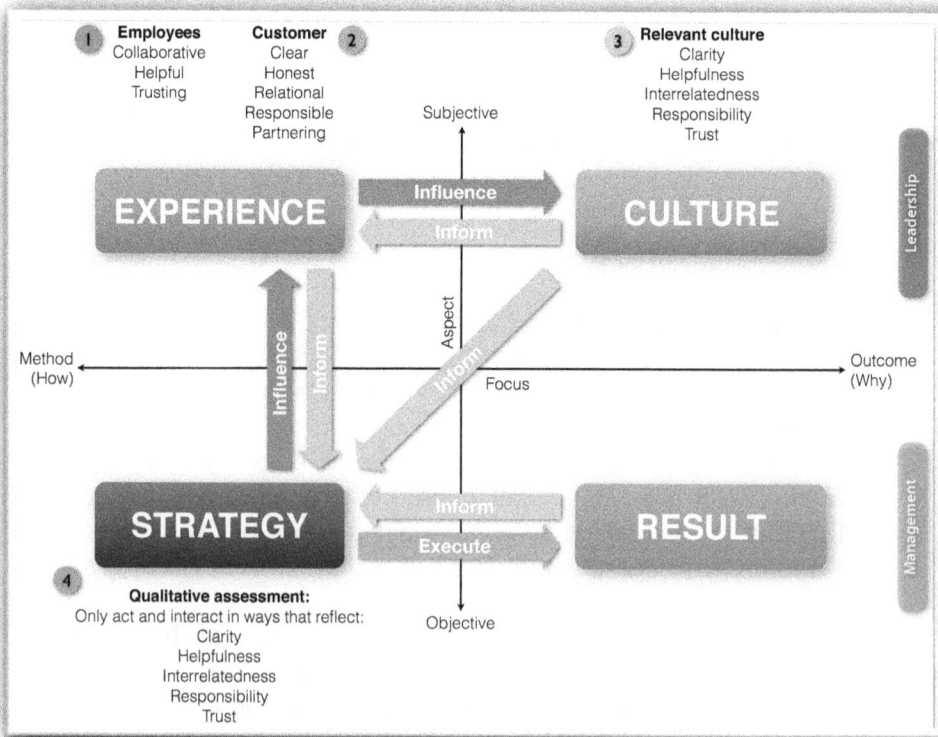

A simplified example based on an actual scenario.

What is cultural leadership?

Stacking the 8 factors of cultural influence in your favour

As each stage of cultural maturity progresses, it takes with it the positive and productive use of all the stages before it. Mind you, the not so helpful aspects will still occur — within limits.

The eight factors of cultural leadership and influence

Evolution is additive and integrative. Each culture stage also reveals one or more factors of cultural leadership and influence that are involved in the creation, maintenance and change of culture. The six evolving stages of culture maturity reveal that there are eight factors involved in culture. Most research and books into culture and culture change refer to one or more of these eight factors.

What we've found is that these eight factors are always active all the time, whether we're aware of them or not. These eight cultural influence factors are 'how' culture is changed and optimised — because they already created it. Though they're always active, we're not always aware of them nor are we necessarily always being responsible for them even when we are.

There are many possible attributes of effective leadership. To develop greater leadership effectiveness is to work on and develop those attributes. In other words, those attributes of effective leadership are your strategy for greater leadership effectiveness.

These eight factors of cultural leadership, influence and change are your strategy for leading, influencing and changing culture. The eight factors are the attributes of cultural leadership and change.

That the eight factors of cultural influence are the strategy for culture change, is shown in the following diagram and are described in this section.

Subjective

EXPERIENCE →Influence→ ←Inform← CULTURE

Leadership

Aspect

Method (How) ←——————→ Outcome (Why)

Focus

Influence / Inform / Inform

Ineffective	Factor	Effective
Stagnated	ORGANISATION	Regenerated
Fragmented	STRATEGY	Integrated
Limited	ENGAGEMENT	Distributed
Misaligned	BEHAVIOUR	Aligned
Disconnected	PROMOTION	Reinforced
Unused	STANDARD	Confirmed
Undermined	CONVERSATION	Upheld
Blocked	AWARENESS	Received

Inform

Execute → RESULT

Management

Objective

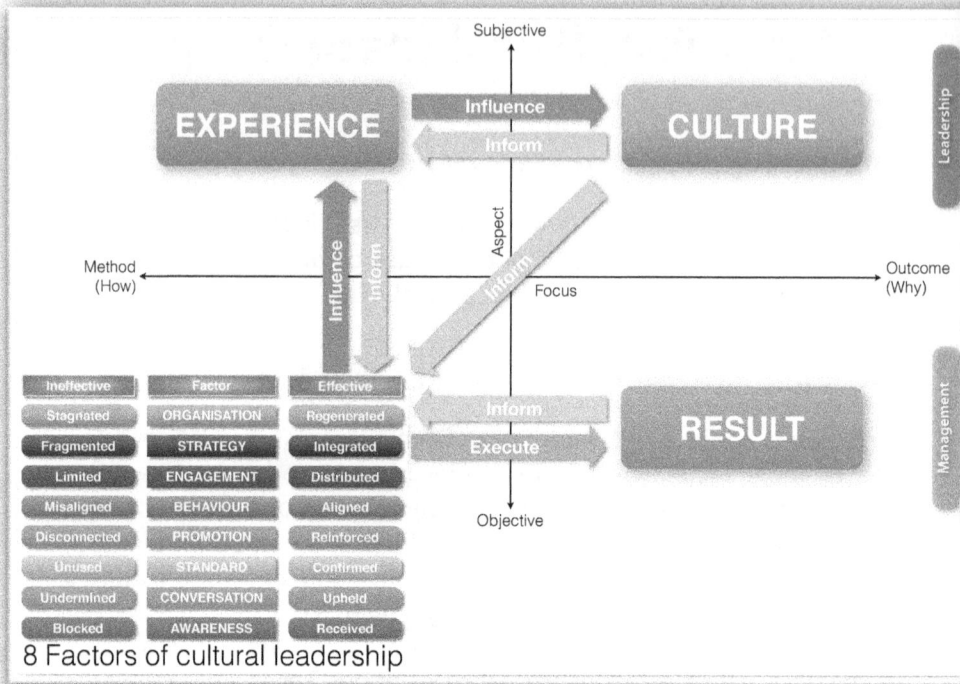

8 Factors of cultural leadership

The 8 Factors of cultural leadership and influence **are** the integrated strategy for continuous culture regeneration.

A healthy and effective continuum

The less aware and responsible you are with these eight factors, the more likely your culture will be misaligned with what it needs to be — and the more likely it'll be unhealthy and ineffective. The more aware and responsible you are with these eight factors, the more likely your culture will be aligned with what it needs to be — and the more likely it'll be healthy, effective and optimally productive.

A culture is ineffective when all factors are stacked away from and misaligned with the optimal standards. The more factors that are misaligned and the further away from standard they are, the more the culture will be hindering the strategic objectives of the organisation, making the results increasingly less likely.

A culture is effective and heathy when all factors are stacked towards and aligned with the optimal standards. The more factors that are aligned and the closer to standard they are, the more the culture will be helping the strategic objectives of the organisation, making the results more likely.

Origin and health requirements for the eight factors

Using Stage 1's uncontrolled chaotic impulse

The chaotic stage of cultural maturity is all about reactive impulse — it reveals the need for awareness of when standards are breached and reached.

Every culture will raise an impulse whenever there's a departure from what it regards as important. That impulse is the awareness raising alarm system of the culture. In a dysfunctional culture, it's an awareness system that's usually blocked and covertly propagates its own dysfunction.

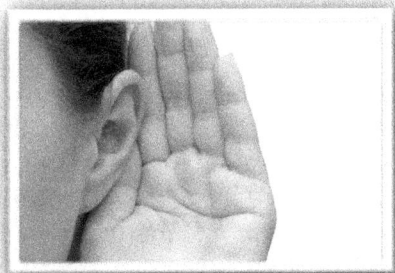

Its positive use is when this impulse is in response to and supports the desired productive culture. The impulse then becomes part of a health-promoting cultural immune system — by being promoted as positive examples.

Awareness is a prerequisite to action. In this case, the impulse is surfaced and received in a way that reflects and supports the desired productive culture.

Awareness is ineffective and unhealthy when experience is compromised, resisted and blocked. It's effective and healthy when valued experience is received and accurately identified.

Using Stage 2's de facto responsiveness

The de facto stage of cultural maturity is all about the culture that's created as influential people respond in an environment where there's an undefined or not enacted standard — it reveals the need to address through conversation any situations that are 'below standard' and to do so whenever they are.

Impulse provides awareness of deviations from the prevailing standard. In a high functioning culture, this impulse provides immediate awareness of deviations from the desired productive culture — an awareness that can be shared with others.

Once there's awareness, it's possible to respond appropriately to departures — to draw attention to that through conversation. In this case, the response itself needs to exemplify and uphold the desired productive culture.

Conversation is ineffective and unhealthy when it ignores misalignment with standard, thwarts those in alignment, or deals with deviations from standard in ways that undermines the standard.

It is effective and healthy when situations that are below standard are addressed, is itself done in a way that demonstrates the standard being addressed, and is used to bring attention to and reinforce when standards are met.

Using Stage 3's promoted aspiration

The promoted stage of cultural maturity is all about creating awareness of the desired standard — it reveals the need for a standard that's connected with the work and workplace and promoted in ways that reinforce that standard.

It's important that people are aware of the productive culture that is desired. Publishing that aspiration sends a powerful message. It reinforces the message in an environment where the productive culture is experienced in a positive way. It breeds cynicism in an environment where the espoused culture remains largely unused.

Rather than discrete, potentially misaligned events, there's an acknowledgement that everyone is continually participating in the creation of culture. Every interaction is considered as a possible event for participation. The motto of this stage is, 'We are all participants in the culture of our own making.'

An espoused and published aspiration declares what people are working towards. It also gives context to what is a departure to become aware of, and conditions what it means to exemplify standards. Promoted aspiration reveals what happens when situations are below standard, and confirms what above standard looks like. It also demonstrates that the standard is in use.

The standard is ineffective when it remains unused, values are ignored and the de facto standard prevails. It's effective when the standard is regularly used as a qualitative and behavioural reference and therefore confirmed. It's most effective when it reflects the valued experience of both employees and customers.

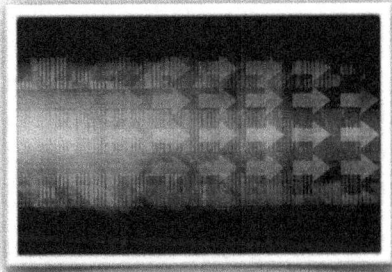

Promotion is ineffective and unhealthy when it is disconnected from the work and the workplace, creating irrelevant experiences and mixed messages. It's effective and healthy when promotional events and practices use case-studies, and stories to reinforce the standard.

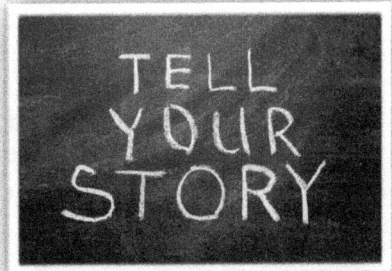

Using Stage 4's modelled responsibility

The modelled stage of cultural maturity is all about individuals engaging with the optimal standard — it reveals the need to identify and align behaviour with the innate values of the people involved and for ensuring that individual engagement with aligned behaviour is widely distributed.

Individually and in groups, people intrinsically engage with their actual values. It's important that individual behaviour be aligned and that engagement not be limited to a few people, but distributed throughout the organisation.

Individuals accept their responsibility for their part in a culture of their own making. They assume leadership. They choose to participate in every interaction according to the desired productive cultural aspiration, and surface and respond to departures — their own or others — in a way that demonstrates it.

When Individuals lead and consistently apply themselves to the desired productive culture, it becomes the addressed standard. When it occurs, it is recognised, reinforced and supported. Failure to do so is recognised and responded to in a way that itself demonstrates the desired standard, thereby reinforcing it.

41

Behaviour is ineffective and unhealthy when misaligned with the standard and when people model inappropriate behaviour. It's effective and healthy when people show individual leadership and align their own values in a way that models the standard.

Engagement is ineffective when groups model the problem and malign people who model the standards. It's effective then modelling of the standards is widely distributed and groups productively align with their own innate values in upholding those standards.

Using Stage 5's aligned optimisation

The aligned stage of cultural maturity is all about aligning an engaged staff culture with the valued experience of the customer — it reveals the need to identify what the valued customer experience actually is, use that valued experience as part of the required standard and then to engage in distributed alignment with that.

Using Stage 6's integrated and seamless transformation

The integrated stage of cultural maturity is all about ensuring the more fixed aspects of the work and workplace are brought into alignment with the valued customer experience — it reveals the need for all elements of the **strategy** to be integrated and for the organisation to regenerate seamlessly.

The insistence that the desired productive cultural standard be upheld becomes so strong that all elements of the work and workplace are assessed according to the presence or departure from that standard. Systems, structures and processes characterise and reinforce the productive culture.

When effective and healthy, people are not so much seeking to become aware of and align with the productive culture. They already do so, unconsciously, reliably, and seamlessly. It's no longer about shaping the culture as much as being shaped in a self-generating way. Not so much using as being used in service of something greater — it's the vehicle for one's legacy.

Strategy is ineffective and unhealthy when fragmented and producing inconsistent and incompatible experience of the work and workplace. It's effective and healthy when integrated in a way that aligns the organisations structures, systems, work and work design in a way that optimises valued experience.

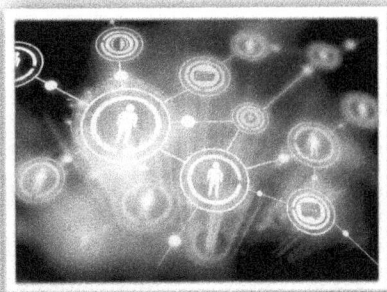

Organisation is ineffective and unhealthy when there's stagnant neglect or legitimate ignorance of valued experience and the factors that influence it. It's effective and healthy when there's a stewardship-like responsible commitment to optimising the culture through continuous and complete regeneration.

Factoring in stages

The six stages of cultural maturity and approach to culture change reveal the eight factors and attributes of cultural leadership and influence. The six stages and the eight factors that they reveal are summarised as follows:

Stage 6: Integrated	Organisation and Strategy
Stage 5: Aligned	Standards
Stage 4: Modelled	Behaviour and Engagement
Stage 3: Promoted	Promotion
Stage 2: De facto	Conversation
Stage 1: Chaotic	Awareness

The next two sections — recipe for disaster and recipe for success — highlight the importance and role of these eight factors of cultural influence in creating a culture that's misaligned or aligned with what it needs to be.

Recipe for disaster (ineffective cultural leadership)

If you want to create a chronically dysfunctional or misaligned culture, frustrate clients and disengage staff, do the following:

1. Block **awareness** by resisting knowing when valued experience is breached and reached.
2. Undermine the optimal standard and establish a de facto standard through **conversation** that ignores misalignment, thwarts when actions are aligned, and itself does not reflect the desired standard.
3. Ensure the defined **standard** remains unused, values are ignored and that the de facto standard prevails.
4. Send mixed messages and provide irrelevant experiences by **promoting** a desired standard in a way that's disconnected with the work and the workplace, and is itself regarded as irrelevant.
5. Allow individuals to be misaligned and model inappropriate **behaviour** outside of normal limits.
6. Provide the conditions for limited **engagement** by ignoring when groups model the problem and disrupt when the experience of behaviour is aligned.
7. Have a fragmented **strategy** that provides an incompatible and inconsistent experience of the work and workplace.
8. Cultivate **organisational** stagnation by ignoring people's experience and need for visible and qualitative completeness.

Besides, when a culture is highly misaligned with what it must be, this is already happening, as summarised in the following table.

Create dysfunction	Ineffective	Factor
Neglect of people's complete experience	Stagnated	ORGANISATION
Incompatible experience of work & workplace	Fragmented	STRATEGY
Groups model problem and malign the aligned	Limited	ENGAGEMENT
Individuals model inappropriate behaviour	Misaligned	BEHAVIOUR
Mixed messages and irrelevant experiences	Disconnected	PROMOTION
Values ignored and de-facto standard prevails	Unused	STANDARD
Misaligned is ignored and aligned is thwarted	Undermined	CONVERSATION
Valued experience compromised and resisted	Blocked	AWARENESS

It's a recipe for cultural disaster when all factors are stacked in an ineffective, misaligned way.

Recipe for success (effective cultural leadership)

If you want to create an optimally functional and aligned culture, delight clients and engage staff, do the following:

1. Receive **awareness** by decoding and identifying when valued experience is breached and reached.
2. Uphold the optimal standard through **conversation** that addresses misalignment, recognises and rewards when actions are aligned, and itself reflects the desired standard.
3. Ensure the relevant **standard** is actively confirmed by referencing examples of when valued experience is reached and breached.
4. Send consistent messages and provide relevant reinforcement by **promoting** examples of the optimal standard in a way that connects people with the standard at work and in the workplace.
5. Support individuals to be aligned and model appropriate **behaviour** in a way that honours their personal values.
6. Provide the conditions for distributed **engagement** by orienting groups around what already innately engages them and supports the positive expression of their individual values.
7. Have an integrated **strategy** that provides a compatible and consistently valued experience of the work and workplace.
8. Cultivate **organisational** regeneration through stewardship of necessary principles and people's complete experience.

Besides, when a culture is positively aligned with what it must be, this is already happening, as summarised in the following table.

Factor	Effective	Create optimal function
ORGANISATION	Regenerated	Complete qualitative transformation
STRATEGY	Integrated	Aligning organisation and work design
ENGAGEMENT	Distributed	Group values support productive engagement
BEHAVIOUR	Aligned	Individual values support optimal standard
PROMOTION	Reinforced	Case-studies, stories, events and practices
STANDARD	Confirmed	Valued experience identified and referenced
CONVERSATION	Upheld	Values-based conversations and feedback
AWARENESS	Received	Decoding and identifying valued experience

It's a recipe for cultural success when all factors are stacked in an effective, aligned way.

To work continually and to continually work on

All eight factors of cultural leadership and influence are always active — either towards ineffective misalignment or effective alignment with what it must be. Left alone, they're unlikely to be optimal, and may even be continuously working against your strategy. Working intentionally and skilfully with those factors — showing effective cultural leadership — changes things in support of your strategy.

Awareness, conversation, standards, and promotion are continuous factors — they're the micro elements that are always occurring and can change and become more effective with practise. Behavioural alignment, distributed engagement, integration of strategy and organisational regeneration are ongoing factors — they're the macro elements that are always happening and can change and become more effective with regular attention and focus. Both the micro and macro factors of effective cultural leadership may be helped with specialist coaching, support and training.

The eight micro and macro factors of Continuous Culture Regeneration™, the complete approach for effective cultural leadership, their ineffective and effective dimensions, and what they're generally about when optimally effective, is summarised in the following diagram.

	Ineffective	Factor	Effective	About
Macro	Stagnated	ORGANISATION	Regenerated	Complete transformation
	Fragmented	STRATEGY	Integrated	Aligning work and workplace
	Limited	ENGAGEMENT	Distributed	Group values and purpose
	Misaligned	BEHAVIOUR	Aligned	Individual values and purpose
Micro	Disconnected	PROMOTION	Reinforced	Stories, examples, practices
	Unused	STANDARD	Confirmed	Identifying strategic culture
	Undermined	CONVERSATION	Upheld	Conversations and feedback
	Blocked	AWARENESS	Received	Decoding valued experience

Continuous Culture Regeneration™ and effective cultural leadership integrates all factors of cultural influence towards optimal function.

How do I put culture to work?

Roadmap for continuous culture regeneration

Continuous culture regeneration

Getting and staying fit takes work. It is not a single event. It takes regular, ongoing attention, focus and work. The effects of exercise are cumulative. Getting unfit is easy — all you need to do is do nothing.

All practise is like that. Each time we act is like putting air into a balloon with a slow leak. The balloon can easily be allowed to go flat — all it takes is to do nothing — it is the reliable and predictable result of neglect. For it to remain full and expand, the ballon requires regular attention.

Practise is about cumulative, ongoing effect — it's infinite. When we're playing an infinite game, it's what we do every day that determines the trajectory of what we're creating. Infinite is not start-stop — it's ongoing.

Culture is like that. Culture is ongoing. Culture is continuous practise. Culture is cumulative.

Culture, leadership, and cultural leadership are all disciplines of ongoing, continuous practise whose effects are iterative and cumulative.

Continuous culture **stagnation** is continuous work — you may not realise it is a dynamic that is already happening continuously. Indeed, it can simply be the natural result of inaction.

Continuous culture regeneration is continuous work — it takes deliberate focus and practise for it to happen continuously. What matters is that the factors are stacked towards healthy regeneration.

Either way the factors of cultural leadership and influence are at work continuously and changing culture is continuous work. It's work at all levels of your organisation — individual, team and organisational.

Implementing cultural leadership and influence

There's a certain logic to working with the eight factors of cultural influence.

As such, a possible way of layering in and working with the eight factors of continual and ongoing cultural influence is as follows:

1. **Awareness.** Understand the dynamics of culture and identify the valued experience of the people involved.

   a. **Customers.** Decode and identify the valued experience of your customers as it is already.

   b. **Employees.** Identify the individual and group values that your people, groups and teams innately already engage around.

   c. **Stakeholders.** Decode and identify the valued experience of your stakeholders as it is already.

2. **Standards.** Identify what your optimal culture must be. This is the standard you align to. You'll know what it is when it's so self-evident that it seems like you don't really have a choice.

3. **Promotion.** Promote the standards that are relevant for a given group and the organisation. Identify examples of when individual and group standards met or sustainably exceeded the valued customer experience and establish practises where those stories are shared and told.

4. **Strategy.** Use your cultural aspiration as the ongoing basis for the qualitative assessment of your existing strategy, the eight factors of cultural influence, and for regular progress reviews.

5. **Conversation.** Learn how to give values-based opinion and feedback and have effective values-based conversations.

6. **Behaviour.** Identify your own and support your people to identify their orienting values and how you translate that to the healthy expression of your behaviour.

7. **Engagement.** Identify your group values that teams already innately engage with and how they translate that to the healthy

expression of how people in those teams function, how their personal values support the group engagement, and how the group values and behaviours support the cultural standard.

8. Organisation. Apply your defining values to optimise your culture through continuous regeneration, transforming your existing situation, organisation, and market — making that your enduring legacy. Remember it's not a single event, project or program. It's about being disciplined in elevating all the eight factors of cultural influence towards what they must be in an ongoing way. Then you have both the objective and subjective aspects of transformation working together in a complete approach to change — making successful adaptation more likely.

The need for method integrity

Respect can't result from denigration. Exclusion won't create inclusion. No form of prejudice can ever produce equality.

When it comes to the subjective, intangible, invisible aspects of people and human experience, the outcome you're after must be the method you use.

Respect and inclusion are created when the methods are consistently experienced overall as being respectful and inclusive. The methods of respectfulness and inclusion influence the outcome of respect and inclusion. In other words, **the end is the method.**

A crucial and often overlooked aspect of culture change and organisational transformation initiatives is how the change and transformation project is itself experienced — and whether the change methods used are congruent with the intended outcome.

For example, declaring and imposing a standard of collaboration and inclusion on people is more likely to reinforce a culture of authority and control — which is fine if that's what's you're after. The gap between the espoused 'collaboration and inclusion' and the experienced 'authority and control' is a problem. From the perspective of the intended outcome, the method lacks integrity.

What matters is that the methods used reflect and are experienced according to the intended outcome. **The culture you're after informs the method needed to achieve it.** As such, any culture change initiative needs to be self-referential — be done in a way that models the culture it intends to produce. Only then, from a cultural perspective, is there method integrity.

Culture change projects need method integrity.

Leading cultural change

In *Leading Change*, John Kotter shows that 70% of major organisational change efforts fail. To successfully adapt, he defines an eight step process for effectively leading workplace change.

Though the eight steps describe what to do, it's as important that change be done with method integrity — to do change in a way that demonstrates and models the envisioned culture. To lead cultural change with method integrity, these eight steps need to include, reflect and model the eight factors of cultural leadership and influence. Kotter's change process updated into seven integrated steps with the eight factors of cultural influence that enliven them:

1. Establish a sense of urgency[6] (WHY). People are convinced of the importance and need to act when they accept *why* the need for change. Usually defined in terms of the need to adapt to changing external circumstances, this step is all about *why* change is needed. However, *why* is due to both external and internal circumstance and feedback. *Why* is the need to successfully adapt externally and to effectively integrate internally. *Why* is the desired combined outcome — of culture and results. It's having awareness of and promoting the relevant cultural standard a group must be as part of their best **strategy** to achieve their results. *Why* goes with *vision*.

2. Develop a change vision[6] (VISION). A vision is a desired outcome, a why, that direct efforts. Strategy provides pathways for achieving outcomes. Usually defined in concrete terms, a complete vision describes both aspects of the intended outcome — the strategically relevant cultural standard and tangible results. The optimal **strategy** is the pathway for both. *Vision* goes with *why*.

3. Communicate vision for buy-in[6] (COMMUNICATE). Communication is continuous though not always explicit nor intentional. What matters is people accept and engage with the vision and standards they reflect, and the strategy to achieve them. Ensure the experience of vision promotion reflects and demonstrates the vision. Promote positive examples of standards reached. Communicate messages so they reflect and model the envisioned standard — or risk cynicism and a lack of acceptance. Acceptance is more likely when the micro factors are aligned and congruent with the standard — there's recognised awareness of the relevant standard whose **promotion** reflect and reinforce it, and formal and informal conversation continually uphold it.

4. Never let up[6] (**PERSIST**). Use the legitimacy and credibility born of relevance and change success to consistently adjust the macro factors towards the standards and vision. Ensure ongoing **strategy** integration — systems, structures, processes — that support more aligned behaviour and increasingly distributed engagement.

5. Create the guiding coalition[6] (INFORM TEAMS). Usually defined as forming a sufficiently influential 'change team' to lead the broader change effort, this step is really about all teams engaging with the effective execution of their combined strategy. Informing teams means every team in the organisation knows why and how to do their part — to create the subculture their team must be to best produce their intended results. Effective influence is when team members engage in behaviour and conversation that recognise and reward, reflect and reinforce, their intended team subculture.

6. Empower broad-based action[6] (EMPOWER PEOPLE). Legitimise change by dealing with inhibiting influences and changing — in a way that reflects the standards — systems and structures so they support and reinforce the change. Ensure an integrated **strategy** encourages aligned behaviour and distributed engagement.

7. Generate short-term wins[6] (INFORM PROGRESS). Reinforce the standard by promoting examples of achievement and success. Integrate changes into the **strategy** by ensuring systems recognise and reward people who engage with aligned behaviour.

8. Incorporate changes into culture[6] (NORMALISE ORGANISATION). Changes easily revert to old ways unless they reflect new social norms and shared assumptions. **Persistence** and communication are needed. Anchor changes in workplace culture by connecting them with successes. Develop the means for ongoing organisational renewal through cultural leadership development and succession. Keep going until the changes stick — until the organisation regenerates itself and its culture according to the new standards — and the envisioned changes are the new norm.

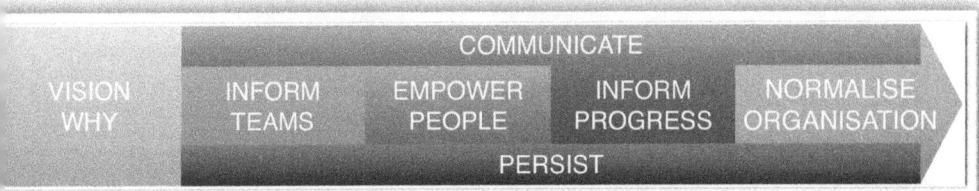

COMMUNICATE				
VISION WHY	INFORM TEAMS	EMPOWER PEOPLE	INFORM PROGRESS	NORMALISE ORGANISATION
PERSIST				

The seven step process for leading cultural change.

How do I lead and influence more skilfully?

From knowledge of factors to skilful action

Integrated learning is still sequential

The eight factors of cultural leadership and influence are a learnable, integrated and complete set. Each factor on it's own could be regarded as an otherwise discrete and learnable skill — and in many ways, each of them are.

However, while that is partially true, each factor already supports the others in creating culture, so each must be recognised and practised as part of a complete approach. Though it would be sub-optimal to address each factor and learn each skill in isolation, the fact is that skills are learned and practised in sequence.

What matters is having an interrelated and mutually reinforcing set of skills that we progressively build on. We learn and practise those skills in sequence.

To optimally align and change culture, we need to continually effectively lead and optimally influence culture. To lead and influence culture we need to skilfully put into practise the eight factors of cultural leadership and influence. To do that well means first learning how to put those skills into practise, and then doing the practise.

The eight factors of cultural leadership and influence reveal what needs to be learned and practised to effectively lead and skilfully influence cultural change.

The practise of cultural leadership and change are learnable skills.

Factoring in skilful practise

Each of the eight factors of cultural leadership and influence have one or more areas of discrete and learnable skill that together form a complete and integrated approach. These factors and their learnable skills are outlined as follows:

1. Awareness by identifying and assessing situational values.

2. Standards through values identification and integration.

3. Promotion by applying the values promotion framework.

4. Strategy utilising **qualitative assessment and work design**.

5. Conversation using values-based feedback and conversation.

6. Behaviour via personal values identification and alignment.

7. **Engagement** with **group values identification and alignment** and **complete employee engagement**.

8. Organisation from complete visible and qualitative transformation.

This is summarised in the following table. It shows each factor of cultural leadership and influence, what the effective and healthy aspect of each factor is about, and what the practise is to lead and influence each of them skilfully.

Factor	Effective	About	Skilful leadership practise
ORGANISATION	Regenerated	Complete transformation	Complete tangible and qualitative transformation
STRATEGY	Integrated	Aligning work and workplace	Values-based assessment and work design
ENGAGEMENT	Distributed	Group values and resilience	Group values alignment & complete engagement
BEHAVIOUR	Aligned	Individual values and purpose	Personal values identification and alignment
PROMOTION	Reinforced	Stories, examples, practices	Values promotion framework
STANDARD	Confirmed	Identifying strategic culture	Complete values identification and integration
CONVERSATION	Upheld	Conversations and feedback	Values-based feedback and conversation
AWARENESS	Received	Decoding valued experience	Identify and assess situational values

The 8 Factors of cultural leadership and their corresponding practises to influence them skilfully.

Conclusion

Congratulations—you've finished this book and the introduction to effective cultural leadership and influence using the strategic culture dynamics model™ and the continuous culture regeneration method™.

Worthy work

Working well with culture is worthy work, though it's far more work if you don't work it well.

The continuously successful adaptation and regeneration of your organisation is the holy grail of culture change. It's not a one-off event or project. It is the result of continuous and effective cultural leadership. It's about being externally adaptive and internally integrative — optimally, strategically and relevantly.

If you integrate these eight factors of cultural leadership and influence in an effective and healthy way then you're stepping into intentional continuous culture regeneration — culture change aligned with valued customer experience that engages employees. You are moving from dysfunction to optimal function. You're using the best of each stage of cultural evolution as part of an integrated approach that stacks all factors of cultural leadership and influence in favour of the culture you must be more of to maximise the likelihood of achieving your intended results.

Unless

That is of course unless you're not up for the collective responsibility and leadership that it requires and then all you can do is continue to invest precious time, energy and resources in managing problems and needlessly stepping on what the customer and staff truly value.

Achieving continuous culture regeneration is continuous focus, work and practise. What matters is that your practise be progressing ever increasingly towards the effective and healthy expression of all eight factors of cultural leadership and influence. It matters that you're heading in the right direction.

The first step is up to you. You have to believe it is possible and step into the practise of becoming and creating who you must be to succeed.

Effective responsibility

I won't tell you what your culture should be — I'll help you discern and decide for yourself who you must be. I won't use research to persuade you to be like someone else — I'll help you use what your own environment is already telling you and to be in conviction about what's right for you.

I'm at my best when I help you realise your own insights in a way that is empowering for you and your people. What will not work for me is if I try to 'tell' you what you, your team, or your culture should be. That would not be your insight — though I can help you discover for yourself and act on your insight once you have it.

Nor will I tell you what the 'right' interpretation of your experience is, for I trust that you come to your own conclusion. I may suggest alternative interpretations, but you are the one who decides. Besides, you're the one who lives with your decisions every day and feels the pressure to constantly adapt.

You are the responsible authority on what your culture must be — you are even if you don't yet know what that is. To help you with that, I've developed methods through which you can gain insight into your own situation in a way that helps you make better and more effective decisions — decisions that illuminate, liberate and empower you towards sustainable achievement. I do this to help you realise and act on what your situation shows you must become more of to optimise your success.

I enjoy helping people align with what their situations already show they must become. Besides, it's the people in a situation who are responsible for what they do about it.

I don't know at the outset what your culture needs to be — but I do trust that you can work together and specifically clarify what you must be. What I do know is that your culture must become more strategic and relevant if you're to continue to deliver the valued experience for the people that matter for your ongoing success.

Adaptively

As you participate with your teams and organisations, I have three wishes for you:

Aware: That you decipher your own situation, discover who you must become to be most successful, and effectively lead that into being. It's not about trying to get it right or perfect, just clear enough in a way that resonates for you and that's embedded in your work and workplace.

Act: That you put into action and effectively lead what you realise and discover. You won't really know how relevant your strategic culture is until you put it to action. Others will let you know when you receive what they're saying about their valued experience. Like the old saying goes — be who you are and the world will give you feedback.

Adapt: That you pay attention to what improves your leadership and to what happens for you and others when you act. This is your feedback that informs your ability to improve what you do and how you go about it. Bring your strategically relevant culture to life and remain flexible about how you do so. Cultural leadership, like all leadership, is adaptive.

Let me know

I'd love to hear about how you go and how this has helped, or how I may be able to help. I'd enjoy adding the story of your journey, experience and success to a growing library of examples.

Send me a message through philip@philipoudevrielink.com. Visit www.philipoudevrielink.com for additional resources. Sign-up to my newsletter to stay in touch and to be notified of programs.